Written by W.L. Whittington

Illustrated by Tom Farr

Young
Rock Collector's
GUIDE TO THE
UNIVERSE

FORWARD

This book was created to help fan the flame of enthusiasm for young rock collectors- some of whom may grow up to be renowned geologists!

I believe that even the most mature readers of this book will get caught up, as I did, in the wonderful story of our planet's formation.

It is a story whispered to our scientists from dark caves and deep mines by the rocks themselves.

Tom Farr

TABLE OF CONTENTS

WE LIKE ROCKS!

Hi, I'm the "Rock Guy," and sometimes I think all rocks are magnets. That's because I feel a "tug" whenever and wherever I see an unusual or colorful rock! It's like the rock is saying, "hey, pick me up!"

Maybe you love rocks like I do. If so, then this book is for you!

In the next few pages our friends, the rocks, will tell us many secrets. You are probably thinking, ***"What, rocks can talk?"*** Well the scientists who study them will tell you that they do! But these scientists have to work really hard and listen carefully to hear what rocks have to say. And WOW! ***...THE STORIES ROCKS TELL ARE AMAZING!***

Did you know rocks taught the scientists much of what they know about how the dinosaurs died? We are going to learn what happened to the dinosaurs in this book. Rocks also have secrets we can learn about ***things*** from outer space, like asteroids, and meteors, and comets. Hey, while we're at it, we'll even discover what the rocks have to tell us about those big, scary, hot, loud, fiery mountains known as ***volcanoes.***

This book is just loaded with so many cool things that I can't wait to get started! But first, here are some things to look for as you read:

- How rocks got here in the First place
- How our planet earth was formed
- Why the dinosaurs disappeared
- Lots of pictures of my favorite rocks, gems, and minerals, and their names.
  (If you got this book with my Extreme Rock and Fossil Kit…available on Amazon, you can use it to help identify the rocks in your kit).

I'm not a scientist, but a rock collector like you. Over many years, I've learned a lot about rocks and the lessons they teach us. I'm hoping that you enjoy rocks as much as I do.

IT ALL BEGAN
WITH A BANG!

Let's start as close to the beginning as we can. Scientists tell us that at the beginning there was a really big bang. What caused the "Big Bang" is something scientists have guesses about, but they really can't tell us much for sure. Another word for "bang" is explosion.

This explosion turned empty space into billions and billions of stars like our own star. We call our star the Sun.

Plus, there were all kinds of gases and rocks formed by the "Big Bang". Our earth was made from these gases and rocks.

Have you ever seen the fireworks at a 4th of July celebration? Did you notice all the bits and pieces of paper flying outward when firecrackers popped? Imagine that the Big Bang must have been something like that, only so much bigger.

There were pieces of fiery matter and gases zooming outward away from the bang. And guess what! Those burning rocks are still zooming outward into deep space, because the Big Bang is still happening. Stars like the ones we see in the sky at night, are all zooming out to the edges of space. This means that the universe gets bigger and bigger every second.

THE BIG BANG!

Have you ever seen someone blowing up a balloon that gets bigger and bigger and bigger as it fills with air? That is sort of like our universe would look if you could watch it expanding.

But what about the rocks? Let's get back to the rocks. You could think of stars as gigantic rocks, I guess, if the rocks were so hot they were on fire. But really, our star, the sun, and all the other stars are mostly made of two burning gases: helium and hydrogen. It's also made of a very tiny amount of metal.

And, the two gases aren't burning in the way that we see things burn on earth. The sun's gases are creating heat as they join together. It's a process called "nuclear fusion".

That process is not a topic of this book, but the heat from nuclear fusion makes the sun really hot. The sun creates light and energy for the earth. The sun controls the way we live on earth.

OUR SOLAR SYSTEM

Did you notice something odd in this picture of the sun and planets? That's right, ROCKS! Huge rocks, small rocks, all shapes and kinds of rocks. There are plenty of rocks in our solar system. ("solar system" just means all of the planets and rocks that go around and around the sun.)

Compared to the nice round planets, the rocks in the picture almost look like worthless trash floating around in space. But, they play a big role in the story of solar system.

The rocks are called **_asteroids._** Most of the asteroids we see on earth are traveling around and around our sun just like the earth does. We call going around the sun "orbiting" the sun.
Most of the asteroids are orbiting the sun in a path that is just past the planet Mars. They are grouped up all together into the biggest rock collection ever! This collection is called "the Asteroid Belt". There are millions of asteroids traveling in that crowded belt! It's sort of like a busy freeway crowded with fast moving cars. So, lots of times they bump together and bounce away in all different directions.

Maybe you have played marbles and you have watched what happens when a fast moving marble comes crashing against another one and sends it flying away.

Imagine a gigantic asteroid-marble, bigger than your house, crashing against another asteroid the size of a school bus.

When this collision happens, imagine that one asteroid zooms away from the sun, out of the asteroid belt, and deeper into space.

The other asteroid might go in the direction of the sun. When an asteroid hits the sun, what do you think will happen? Have you ever seen the hot coals that burn in a barbeque grill? They get all burned up and turn into ashes, right? Well the sun is many times hotter than a barbeque grill!

So you are probably thinking, "they get burned up". And you are right. The sun is so hot that the asteroid will get turned into hot gas.

IN THE BEGINNING ASTEROIDS WERE EVERYWHERE

Soon after the Big Bang, there were probably many more asteroids in our solar system. And, they were probably bigger than now. Eventually, most of the asteroids remaining in the solar system came to be located in the asteroid belt. You may want to stop and look at the drawing of the solar system in this book. As you can see from the drawing, the Asteroid Belt is located just past Mars.

I am going to tell you how much bigger those early asteroids might have been. But first, we should think together about *__time__*. That's because I have a story to tell you about a really HUGE, TREMENDOUS, GIGANTIC asteroid. The story happened a HUGE, TREMENDOUS, GIGANTICALY long time ago.

We usually don't use words like "tremendous" or "gigantic" to talk about time. Mostly, we use words like long or short to talk about time. An example of long or short is when you are playing with your best friend and you have to stop playing and go home. The time that you were playing feels really short, right?

But if you are waiting at a restaurant for your food to come and you are really hungry, the time feels long, doesn't it? Well "LONG" is the kind of time you should think about when you hear the story of the HUGE, TRE-MENDOUS, GIGANTIC asteroid.

 That's because it happened way, way, way back in the past, before your parents, or your grandparents, or their parents or grandparents were alive.

You know how long it takes you to count to 100, right? But what if you had to count to 100 and you could only say 1 number each year on your birthday? So, if you were 8 years old, you could say "one" on your birthday, but then you would have to wait until you were 9 years old to say "two".

I like for all the young future scientists who read this book to think about time and what "a long time" means. That is because the story about the big rock (or asteroid) that you are going to hear in this book can be a little bit scary. But when you know how long ago it happened, it is not really so scary to us.

And even though it happened so long ago, the big rock (or asteroid), still has a lot to tell the scientists.

So, to know how long ago the big asteroid story happened, you would count up numbers of years and years and years and keep counting for many hundreds, and thousands of numbers until you got to 65,000,000.

That's 65 million years ago. It was long before there were any humans around when the big asteroid showed up on our planet, earth.

Now I need to tell you some other interesting things about our universe before we come to the story of the big asteroid.

But first, here is one more thing I will tell you now. Are you ready, here it is!

But, I am warning you, you are probably going to think I am crazy when I tell you this… THE BIG ASTEROID WAS 6 MILES HIGH AND 6 MILES WIDE WHEN IT ZOOMED THROUGH THE AIR AND PAST THE CLOUDS AND HIT THE GROUND ON EARTH!

To understand how high 6 miles is, let's think of how high the clouds in the sky are each day. The clouds are generally about 3 miles above the ground. So, if a 6 mile high asteroid was sitting in your front yard, the top of it would be twice as high as the clouds that you see.

ACTORS IN A MOVIE
ABOUT THE UNIVERSE

What is your favorite movie? Is it Star Wars? Is it Harry Potter? There are lots of different stories in a movie, and lots of different actors who make the story happen. Well the story of how the universe was formed, how our planet got here, what happened to the dinosaurs, and the story of the big asteroid are kind of like a big movie. So next let's take a look at some of the "actors" in our story about the universe.

The actors are:

- The sun
- The planets in our solar system
- Planet earth
- The earth's crust
- The oceans
- Volcanoes
- Rocks
- Ocean plants
- Land plants
- Dinosaurs
- Humans

As you read this story, watch for these characters. But, first, let's take a moment to think about the sun a little more.

THE SUN IS
THE MAIN ACTOR

The first player in our story is the sun. It's really hot! How hot is the sun? It is so hot that it's not a solid rock. It's made up of burning gases.

Here are some comparisons that helps us understand how hot the sun really is.

**Earth's surface 100 degrees
(a really hot day on earth)**

**Sun's surface 10,000 degrees
(100 times hotter than earth)**

**Sun's center 27,000,000 degrees
(the hottest place in our solar system)**

And, now that we know how hot it is, just what is the sun? We started by talking about "The Big Bang" that sent everything flying outward into the universe in a huge explosion.

The sun was created by the Big Bang. It is incredibly hot and so big that it affects everything in our solar system. It provides us with light, heat and gravity.

These are 3 things that we really need on the earth.

SUNLIGHT. The energy of the sun gives us light to see during the day. At night, without the sun's light, we have darkness so we can sleep. While we are sleeping, some of the sun's light reflects off of our moon and shines on the earth. Moonlight can be so bright that we can see objects clearly when we go outside at night.

HEAT. The heat of the sun provides us with the warmth we need to keep from freezing. But, fortunately we are far enough away from the sun to keep its heat from burning us.

GRAVITY. This is the force used by the sun that pulls on the earth and keeps it from drifting away into outer space. If the sun stopped pulling on the earth, it would drift away. Then we would lose the heat and light that we need.

So, is the sun important to us? Yes, we couldn't live on earth without it.

AND WHAT ARE
THE PLANETS?

Now let's look at how the planets got here (and especially planet earth). After the Big Bang, the planets in our solar system (and that includes the earth),were just a collection of gases and rocks. The Big Bang pushed them to a spot close to the sun.

The earth was just a group of gases and rocks spinning really fast. (4 times faster than today).

Many of the asteroids were still hot from the explosion of the Big Bang. They were in big groups that later formed our planets.

So, as more and more of those hot rocks in the "earth group" got closer and closer together, they melted together into one gigantic solid ball of hot rock. That solid ball was becoming the Planet Earth. Eventually there would be 8 planets in our solar system. Some are solid and some are still mostly gases.

Have you ever seen someone heat chocolate chips on a stove until they become a brown gooey pool? The pool of chocolate could be poured into a bowl. When it cooled down, it would take on the shape of the bowl.

This is sort of like the way planets got formed. But, of course there was no bowl to make the shape. Instead, the spinning motion pulled the hot rocks and gases around and around toward the center of the planet until the big ball was formed.

ROCKS
AND
GASES
Spinning
FASTER
BIG,
HOT
ROCK

It's important to remember that part of our planet is still very hot today. In fact, some of the rocks are still all melted down deep inside the earth. This hot liquid rock is called ***magma.***

When magma comes to the surface of the earth, then we call it **_lava._** Say, that hot lava made me think of an apple pie! That's because when an apple pie first comes out of the oven, the inside of the pie is very, very hot and there is lots of runny liquid around the apples. But there is a crust on top that keeps the hot liquid in.

Sometimes there are holes in the crust of the pie and the hot liquid bubbles up through the holes.

In the same way, our earth has a crust of cooler rock that covers the hot, liquid rock below. When hot lava comes up through cracks in the earth's crust, it forms a mountain that we call a **_volcano._**

There are over 500 active volcanoes around the world today. Most of them are under the Pacific Ocean. Why? Because the Pacific Ocean is 6 miles deep! (That is twice as deep as most of the clouds in the sky are high).
Because the Pacific Ocean is so deep, the earth's crust is thinner there. That makes it easier for liquid rock, (magma), to break through the crust and bubble out as a volcano.

<u>So what about the rocks?</u>

Oh yes, the rocks. We will get to them soon! After all, along with the sun, they are the stars of our book! And remember, the rocks are the ones who helped scientists begin to learn all of the interesting things that we know about the other parts of the universe. So, I'm just saving the best for last! (If you were listening carefully, I hinted at one type of rock we will talk about later…it's the kind of rock made by volcanoes).

BACK TO THE BEGINNING

Because you like rocks like I do, you might be like me in another way as well. I am very curious about how and why things work. And I want to know what makes them do what they do. So let's go back to the beginning again. Let's take a closer look at how our earth (along with the rocks in it and on it), got to be like it is today.

First, billions of years ago, the earth was nothing but one large, hot rock. At that time there was no life at all. That is because it was too hot here on earth.

Also, way back then, the earth was missing two very important things! OXYGEN and WATER. So, where did those come from? I am going to tell you what scientists think.

But first, we should learn how our big, hot earth-rock cooled down enough so that oxygen and water could collect on the surface. (Oxygen is the main ingredient in the air we breathe).

A HARD CRUST

When we think about how the earth cooled down, it helps to remember that hot apple pie again. Remember, at the beginning, the earth was spinning 4 times faster than it spins today. This means that the daytime would only last 3 hours and then it would get dark again.

That fast spinning caused the rocks to clump together into one large group. They were hot and sticky, so when they got close enough to touch, they stuck to each other and formed the earth.

Things had to cool down before life could exist on earth. It was so hot that it took millions of years to cool down. Then, finally, the surface of the earth became cool enough to get hard. That hard surface on earth is the **crust.**

The crust is a thin layer on the outside of the planet. Many times it breaks open at different spots and, kapow! Volcanoes are made! Have you ever sprayed whipped cream out of a can on a slice of pie or a bowl of strawberries? Well that whipped cream is under pressure in the can. It is all packed down so tight in the can that it is always pushing to get out. When you push the button on top, it rushes out.

That is the way the hot liquid rock (magma) is inside the earth. Magma is always trying to escape to the surface of the earth.

Weak spots and cracks in the crust are like the button on a can of whipped cream. The cracks let the hot liquid rock inside get out.

So, the crust cooled down and finally, the earth was ready for water. When the water got here, scientists think that there was so much of it that it covered the entire planet. No continents! There was just deep, dark, lifeless water everywhere.

Today, most of the surface of the earth is still covered by water. And, it's deep water! The oceans are from 3 to 6 miles deep.

So, how did all that water get here? Some scientists think it came from outer space and that it took a long, long time to get that much water here. Millions of years! That is because it was delivered to earth by COMETS! Wow! That makes comets one of the most important things to fly through our solar system.

COMETS

As comets fly across the night sky, they are very bright. They look like they are on fire. They have long glowing tails. For many years, people thought they must be burning as they traveled through the sky.

But now we know that they're not even hot. Instead, they are very cold. A comet is made mostly of ice that reflects the light of the sun. The ice crystals in the comet's body and tail act like millions and millions of mirrors all packed together with the light of the sun shining on them and reflecting back at us.

So, scientists believe that millions and millions of comets hit earth after the crust cooled down some. The hot planet and the heat from the sun melted the ice from the comets into water. This happened so many times that the water covered our planet to make one giant ocean.

DEEP, DARK LIFELESS OCEAN WATER

Nothing was alive in the big ocean in the beginning. But then, life started to appear. It was tiny plant life called plankton. It is still around today and most of it is so tiny you have to look through a microscope to see it. These tiny plants need sunlight in order to make oxygen. It's a chemical process called photosynthesis.

Even though plankton is tiny, everything on earth depends on it to stay alive. That's because these tiny plants give the earth two very important things. First, they help make the oxygen that we breathe. Plankton had to appear on our planet before creatures that live on the land, like dinosaurs and eventually humans, could live.

We needed the oxygen that plankton make so we could breathe.

And second, plankton is food for many of the creatures that live in the ocean. Without plankton, fish would not have food to eat. Without fish, meat-eating sharks would not have food to eat.

Without sunlight, all plants including plankton would die. Then the fish that need plankton for food would die. Then, the bigger sea creatures, like sharks, that eat fish would die. This linking together of one thing needing something smaller in order to have food is like a chain. In fact, we call it the **food chain.**

While we are in the ocean, let's talk about sharks for just a minute. I know that if you like rocks, you might like sharks too! Am I right? We think of sharks as scary and dangerous. And they are! So don't go swimming with sharks! But did you know that we really NEED lots and lots of sharks to live in our oceans?

Why is that? Because sharks eat fish! If there were no sharks, there would get to be so many fish in the ocean that they would eat up all of the plankton. With no plankton, then we would eventually have no oxygen.

With no oxygen, no breathing. That means no land animals and people on our planet. Don't you just love sharks?

Food
chain

ROCKS TO
THE RESCUE

We are still setting the stage for our story about the big rock! Now let's move a little further in time away from the beginning of our planet. So everything was covered with ocean water. Let's fast forward to when dry land started popping up out of the ocean.

It's great for plankton and fish and sharks to have all the ocean water they want. And it is wonderful to have plankton making all of that oxygen needed for breathing. But we can't live in the ocean and we need more than plankton to eat.

Humans and animals need solid land to live on. We also need larger plants and lakes of water ,(not salty like ocean water). We call the kind of water that humans and animals can drink **fresh water.**

Here is where ROCKS first appears in our story. Most of us have seen pictures of the islands of our 50th state, Hawaii. We have seen the beautiful palm trees and sandy beaches. And, we know about the big fiery volcanoes that are found there.

Did you know that the islands of Hawaii were made by magma flowing out of the bottom of the ocean?

That's right, so much of it flowed out of cracks in the earth's crust under the Pacific Ocean that big volcanoes formed and got higher and wider until the islands of Hawaii were created.

The same thing happened all over our planet. Volcanoes formed the dry ground by spitting out hot, liquid magma that cooled into big mountains and slabs of hard rock that we call **lava.**

Scientists think that the largest area of land was formed when a giant meteorite zoomed in from space. It slammed through the ocean and into the earth's crust.

Have you ever seen someone hit a piñata at a birthday party with a bat? Candy comes pouring out, right? Well, that is sort of like what happened many millions of years ago when a meteorite hit the earth. The meteorite, (a gigantic space rock), opened a hole in the crust and hot magma came pouring out. The magma cooled and left a big area of rock that was piled up above the surface of the ocean.

Over long, long periods of time, the big area of land broke into pieces and the pieces moved apart. These big pieces of rock, or **land masses** ,are called **continents**.

Next, more and more millions of years passed. During this time, storms and wind and rain and many, many meteorites came and created dust and dirt so that plants could begin to grow and cover the land. This made more oxygen and plant food.

10s or 100s of millions of years went by. Finally there was so much plant food on earth that land animals could live and get bigger and bigger. They grew so big that they became the huge monsters we call **dinosaurs**. Dinosaur means "terrible lizard".

SO WHERE ARE THE DINOSAURS TODAY?

Have you noticed how everything we talk about in this book takes a long, long time to happen. Also, most of it happened a long, long time ago. Well that is true for dinosaurs too! Everything was going really great for the dinosaurs way back then. You might say they were the kings or rock stars of planet earth! But 65 million years ago, the rocks tell us that something terrible happened on earth…for the dinosaurs that is. Maybe what was terrible for them was good for us though!

Can you imagine trying to drive to a movie with your parents and a big tyrannosaurus comes crashing down the street trying to find lunch? That lunch might be your family. And for dessert, maybe he would eat the people in the cars next to you. The earth might not be such a good place for people if the dinosaurs were still around.

I told you there would be a story about the HUGE, TREMENDOUS, GIGANTIC asteroid. Well now it's time for that story.

65 million years ago the dinosaurs were having a great time. There were vegetarian dinosaur dinner parties and meat eater dinosaur parties going on in every neighborhood. One day, the sun was shining and the birds were singing. It was a beautiful, warm day.

Then, all of a sudden, there was a loud noise like a rocket engine. Then a giant rock (or asteroid) came crashing down through the clouds faster than a rocket. It hit a spot that we now call the Gulf of Mexico. The asteroid was BIG! It was six miles high, and six miles wide.

The big rock hit so hard that it crashed right through the earth's crust. It created the largest volcano that we know of on earth. This volcano spit out a giant cloud of ash that covered the earth like a blanket for a long time.

EARTH BEING STRUCK BY
HUGE METEORITE 65 MYA

the cloud was like a big, thick curtain that blocked the sunlight and kept light from getting to the earth. Without sunlight, all of the plants on land and most plants in the ocean (plankton) died.

So there was not nearly enough oxygen for dinosaurs to stay healthy. Since the plants died, the vegetarian dinosaurs ran out of food and died. Guess who was next? Then the meat eaters died. It didn't take too long before most of the life on earth died. (This included plants and animals.)

But once the cloud of ash went away, plants and animals started growing again. Since there were no dinosaurs around to eat them up, people could grow on the earth also. And, wow! Did those people love rocks! They built tools and jewelry, and money and houses and roads and almost everything you can imagine with rocks.

The Volcanic Ash Cloud Darkens the Earth.

HOT AND HEAVY

There are so many different kinds of rocks! Where did all the beautiful rocks, gems, and minerals come from? Scientist say that many are formed by heat and pressure.

When two minerals are combined by the heat, they form a new mineral or gem. So, where on earth is it hot enough with enough pressure to form minerals?

The answer: below the surface . Down under the crust, rocks are closer to the center of the earth. In the earth's center there is magma, or melted rock. Also, the weight of the land and the water above pushes down on the rock to form incredibly beautiful and useful new rocks.

THE ROCKS CHANGE CONSTANTLY

It takes a long time, but rocks are constantly changing. Rocks that come out of volcanoes are called igneous rocks. Over millions of years, they get broken into tiny grains of sand (sediment),and are washed into the ocean. The sand sinks to the bottom of the ocean. There it is put under great pressure by the weight of miles of water. The sand is then formed into a different kind of rock called sedimentary rock. As more and more layers of sedimentary rock are formed, the layers on the bottom get pushed deeper into the earth and closer the earth's hot core.

When great pressure and heat are applied to them, rocks go through a change to become rock of a new kind. We call them metamorphic rocks. The 3 types of rock below make up what we call the "Rock Cycle".

IGNEOUS ROCKS. (ignited rocks) These come from volcanoes.

SEDIMENTARY ROCKS (from sediment or sand) These are packed together by the weight of the oceans.

METAMORPHIC ROCK. Sedimentary rock changes into harder rock like granite due to the heat and pressure under the earth's surface. (Metamorphosis is a similar word we use to describe the change in a butterfly's life cycle.)

A WORLD OF ROCKS

Today, there are so many new rocks, minerals and gems available that we can create almost anything from them. We use them to make lots of things in our house. These include: the roof; the walls in your bedroom; the floor your feet touch in the morning when you wake up; the pipes that bring in water you use to brush your teeth. Almost everything you use during the day is made from a mineral. The study of the earth and all the rocks, minerals and gems on earth is called geology. You might decide to become a geologist or just a rock collector. Either way, it's an exciting study that can last a lifetime.

YOUR ROCK COLLECTION

If you are reading this book, then you probably have been collecting rocks for a while. Or, perhaps you have received a rock collection that someone gave you as a gift. We hope that you have our rock collection called …

Extreme Rocks and Fossils Kit (available on Amazon)

The following pages will help you identify gems and minerals from any rock collection you may have. We will also give you information about geodes, Herkimer diamonds, meteorites and fossils that may be found in some of our kits.

HOW TO IDENTIFY YOUR ROCKS

The very first thing to do with your rock collection is to sort it. You can gather the rocks together by color. Color is the easiest way to identify rocks from any collection bought in a store. Unfortunately, many different rocks have the same color, and so other observations must be made about the properties of your rocks. The most important property is Hardness. The Mohr's Hardness Scale is a one to ten rating of the hardness of every rock, mineral or gem. So, we can use the hardness scale to help identify rocks that otherwise look similar in color.

For example, both quartz and diamonds can be clear and beautiful. However, diamonds are much harder and are rated at the top of the scale, number 10. But, quartz is much softer at number 7 on the hardness scale. So, a diamond will scratch a piece of quartz. But, white calcite, number 3, will not scratch quartz because it is softer than quartz.

Talc is the softest rock, so we grade it number 1. Most of the rocks in your collection are between 3 and 7 on the hardness scale. Even though quartz is number 7 on the scale, it comes in many colors. It may be purple (amethyst), pink (rose quartz), yellow (citrine), grey (smoky quartz), or clear quartz. Just remember that quartz is harder than most of the other rocks in your collection. It will scratch softer rocks like calcite.

Calcite comes in many colors and is inexpensive for beginning rock collectors. It is easy to find in yellow, blue, reddish, white, orange, green, and shades of brown. You can shop at gem shows and purchase larger samples of calcite at a reasonable cost. Quartz will be more expensive and a good item to ask for at Christmas, birthday, or other special occasions when you get gifts.

You can get the Mohr's Hardness Scale from the internet to help your identify your rocks.

Let me conclude this section on identifying rocks by saying that it is easier for beginning rock collectors to buy a rock collection kit that includes a chart to identify most of the rocks and other specimens by sight.

Identifying rocks other than the ones in your kit begins to get a little more difficult, and requires years of study as a scientist or experience as a collector.

THE EXTREME ROCK AND FOSSIL KIT

In this kit, available on Amazon, you will find lots of unusual specimens that I know you will enjoy. Below is a short list of some of the other rock or fossil specimens you may find in one of our rock collections.

<u>Geodes</u>. Geodes are crystal-filled, volcanic bubbles. The crystals look like diamonds in the sunlight but they are too soft. *See my important note after the next page about how to crack a geode open safely.*

<u>Megalodon Tooth Shards</u>. This is a fragment of a tooth from the prehistoric giant, monster shark that was nearly 60 feet long.

<u>Moroccan Sand Shark Teeth</u>. These smaller teeth are easy to find in the sands of Morocco. There are several in each rock kit.

<u>Indian Arrow Heads</u>. These are new arrowheads made from agate.

<u>Fossil Ammonites</u>. Before there were dinosaurs, there were all kinds of strange creatures in the oceans, including Ammonites. These are wonderful to collect! They contain a beautiful example of the Fibonacci spiral.

<u>Herkimer Diamond</u>. Don't get too excited. These unique pieces of quartz have points on all sides, top and bottom. That's like a diamond. But, while these are rare, they are not hard like diamonds. They are great for your collection. You won't find them in most kits.

<u>Meteorite fragment</u>. Wow! This tiny fragment of a rock that fell from the sky is included in one of our newer kits. These should double the cost of the kit but we include them at no extra cost.

<u>Over 100 Specimens</u>. Of course, the kit includes over a hundred stones, both rough and smooth.

On the next page, you will find a chart which will help you identify rocks in our kit or the rocks in your own collection.

IDENTIFICATION CHART

IMPORTANT. You must open a geode safely. To prevent damage to your eyes, wear safety glasses when striking a geode or any rock. You can buy these at a Dollar Store.

Also, we highly recommend that you place your geode inside a plastic "zip-lock" bag before cracking. this will help protect others from flying fragments and keep you from losing the beautiful pieces of crystal.

MORE ABOUT ROCKS AND FOSSILS

I hope that you have enjoyed this introduction to the world of rocks and how our planet was formed from rocks. If you want to know more about rocks, then you are a candidate for becoming either a serious rock collector or even a geologist.

A geologist is someone who studies the rocks, gems, and minerals of the earth. As a geologist, you might work for a company that uses minerals to create products that we consume everyday all around the world.

Minerals are used to create pipes that bring water into your house. They are used to make the walls, flooring and even roof on your house. They are used to make the pages that this book is written on. Minerals are necessary for life as we know it. If you become a geologist, then you will play an important part in the way people live.

Good luck with your collection!